j520.924 HI87x
Heckart, Barba
Edmond Halley,
his comet $11.95

j PV

4/85

Memphis and Shelby County Public Library and Information Center

For the Residents
of
Memphis and Shelby County

Edmond Halley

The Man and His Comet

by Barbara Hooper Heckart

 CHILDRENS PRESS, CHICAGO

AUTHOR ACKNOWLEDGMENTS

Grateful acknowledgment is given to the staffs of both the Royal Society and the Royal Astronomical Society in London for courtesies given to the author.

PICTURE ACKNOWLEDGMENTS

Historical Pictures Service, Chicago—2, 8, 26 (right)
The Bettman Archive, Inc.—12, 19 (top), 22, 26 (left), 30, 46 (top), 53, 59
Ann Ronan Picture Library—19 (bottom), 33, 39, 46 (bottom), 47, 48,
49 (2 photos), 50, (2 photos), 51 (bottom), 52, 56, 70 (2 photos), 79, 82, 90
Ann Ronan Picture Library and E.P. Goldschmidt & Co., Ltd.—51 (top)
Dennis Milon/Sky and Telescope—97
© 1978 Lowell Observatory and AURA, Inc., Kitt Peak National
Observatory—63
Cover illustration by Len Meents, Portrait of Edmond Halley on page 2.

Library of Congress Cataloging in Publication Data

Heckart, Barbara Hooper.
  Edmond Halley, the man and his Comet.

  Bibliography: p.
  Includes index.
  Summary: Presents the life of the seventeenth-century
scientist who made predictions about the comet which bears
his name and discusses many other important scientific
contributions he made.
  1. Halley, Edmond, 1656-1742—Juvenile literature.
2. Astronomers—Great Britain—Biography—Juvenile
literature. 3. Comets—Juvenile literature. 4. Halley's
comet—Juvenile literature. [1. Halley, Edmond, 1656-1742.
2. Scientists] I. Title.
QB36.H25H43 1984   520'.92'4 [B] [92] 83-24000
ISBN 0-516-03202-X

Copyright © 1984 by Regensteiner Publishing Enterprises, Inc.
All rights reserved. Published simultaneously in Canada.
Printed in the United States of America.

  2 3 4 5 6 7 8 9 10 R 93 92 91 90 89 88 87 86 85 84

Memphis/Shelby County Public Library
And Information Center

For Edmond, because he lived in London; for Mary Lou, because she had faith; for Steve, because he mastered the trick of standing in back and standing beside simultaneously.

Table of Contents

Halley's Comet was photographed in 1910, the last time it was visible from earth.

INTRODUCTION

Halley's Comet will return in 1985.

Only six words, and not very startling ones at that. To those of us reading them in the last decades of the twentieth century, they hardly seem amazing at all.

But just a little over three hundred years ago those words electrified the scientific world. Three hundred years is a *very* long time to us. But for a world that has existed for millions of hundreds of years, a mere three hundred years is not so long at all.

It was in 1682 that a young scientist named Edmond Halley began studying comets in earnest. He had seen a comet in 1680 and the Great Comet of 1682. He had been fascinated by the sky since he was a teenager. He had even decided at the age of sixteen to make his lifework the study of the heavens.

Studying the mysterious ways of comets and learning some remarkable facts about them enabled Edmond to make an astonishing prediction. He said that the Great Comet of 1682 was the same comet people had been seeing for centuries, and that it would return again in 1758.

9

This prediction is what he is most remembered for today, but it was just one of hundreds of accomplishments Edmond Halley made in his long life. His life is worth learning about because of his many discoveries and the influence his work had on people of his own time and on all those who have lived after him.

The seventeenth century (the years between 1600 and 1699) has been called the Century of Genius. Edmond Halley was one of the greatest men of that time. He was honored by many people in his lifetime. The achievement for which he is most remembered happened sixteen years after his death, when his prediction about the return of the comet proved to be correct. From that time on, the famous comet has been known as Halley's Comet, not because he discovered it (as is the usual way comets get named), but because of his sensational prediction.

Halley learned that his comet makes its trip around our sun every seventy-six years. It is due to be seen next by people on earth in November of 1985. It will be visible until 1986. If asked to name a comet, most people can name only Halley's Comet, whether or not they have seen it. It may be the most spectacular comet anyone will ever see in our lifetime.

As famous as Edmond Halley was, it is difficult to learn a great deal about him. Many men of his day kept journals or diaries. Edmond did not, so almost all of what is known about him must be dug out of his scientific works or from what others have learned and written about him. His first name is sometimes spelled "Edmund," but he himself spelled it "Edmond" in his handwritten will. No one now alive knows how he pronounced his surname. It could be pronounced any one of three ways: HAW-ley, HAIL-ey, or HAL-ey. A friend of his wrote it "Hawley," which may have been the way it sounded when he heard it spoken. Even the actual date of his birth is not precisely known. Some give the date as October 29, while others say it was November 8.

While many details of Edmond's private life are not known, enough can be learned about him to make him live again in the twentieth century.

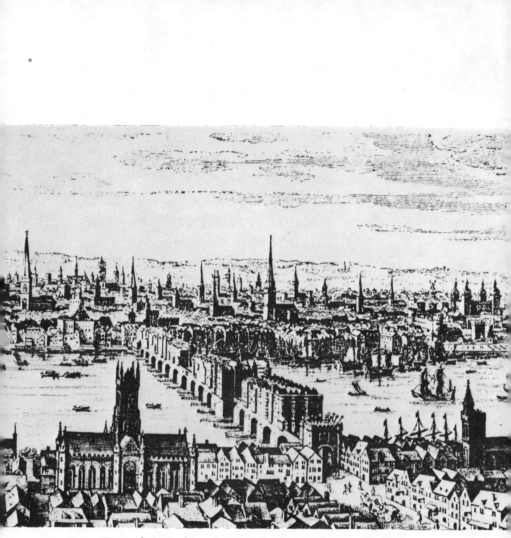

General view of London and the Thames River taken from a plan
dating from the year 1666

Chapter 1

EDMOND HALLEY'S BOYHOOD

Edmond was the son of Edmond Halley and his wife, Anne Robinson Halley. He was born near London, England, probably on October 29, 1656. It was a time of great turmoil in England. Only a few years before Edmond's birth, King Charles I had been beheaded by the followers of Oliver Cromwell, plunging England into a civil war. This war lasted for nearly ten years. It ended when Charles II was brought back from exile and returned to the throne of England.

Edmond's father was a soapmaker and a salter in the heavily populated, grimy city of London. These were not fashionable occupations, but they were essential ones. The work was both dangerous and dirty. Salt was very important for preserving foods in the days before refrigeration. Soap was made from boiling down the carcasses of dead animals, which made dreadful odors, but was essential for cleanliness. Keeping clean was becoming more important, for not too many years after Edmond's birth, bubonic plague ("the Black Death") raged in London. More than 25 percent of the citizens, or one of every four people, died. Many of those who survived did so because they were able to leave the contaminated, crowded, and dirty city of London.

Edmond's father was a wealthy man. He owned property in the city of London and a house in the country, several miles away. It was at the country home that Edmond was born.

Several years after Edmond's birth, a sister, Katherine, was born, but she died as an infant. Another child, a boy named Humphrey, was also born to the Halleys, but he, too, died before he reached adulthood.

Edmond's parents must have grieved at the deaths of their two children, but they were very proud of Edmond. His father recognized early that his son was a very gifted young man. He encouraged him to learn. He had an apprentice teach his son writing and "arithmetique." Edmond took to his lessons with great eagerness.

As a young teenager, Edmond was sent to St. Paul's School, which had been rebuilt after being destroyed in the Great London Fire of 1666. St. Paul's had a reputation for scholarship. The school, still in existence, was over 150 years old before Edmond's father sent him there. Only boys attended school then.

Edmond had winning ways. People enjoyed being around him. He was slender, almost thin, and had brown hair and brown eyes. He was a happy young man and was well liked by both his classmates and his teachers. At the age of fifteen he was appointed captain of the school, a position of honor and respect.

A new master took over at St. Paul's while Edmond was a student there. His name was Thomas Gale. He had been a professor of Greek and had many other interests. He no doubt had great influence on his students, including young Edmond.

Chapter 2

SEVENTEENTH CENTURY PROBLEMS

The boys at St. Paul's School studied Latin, Greek, Hebrew, and mathematics. The latter included geometry, algebra, the art of navigation, and the science of astronomy.

It may seem strange to us in the twentieth century that a school's basic course of study should include navigation. But England needed navigators and people to solve the many practical problems the nation faced. England, being an island, had a large navy both for defending itself against enemies and for exploration. There were English companies that wanted to establish colonies in far-off lands. They also wanted to trade with countries that had products England needed.

Seafaring was a very hazardous undertaking. Once out of sight of land, there was nothing to serve as a landmark. Sailors had compasses, but navigation depended on being familiar with the "landmarks" in the heavens. Sailors had to know everything they could about stars, the planets, and the moon. They needed charts of the stars to be able to sail for weeks out of sight of land and yet be reasonably certain of landing where they intended to land. Tables of locations for stars in the Northern Hemisphere had been made, but they were often filled with errors in the positions of the so-called guiding stars. Different times of the day and different days of the year were also important in determining a correct location at sea.

Ships' captains used compasses, their knowledge of the skies, and their star charts to navigate in the seventeenth century. Small errors in the charts did not matter much when a voyage was short, but the small errors grew larger as the distance of a voyage increased. Only rough estimates of a ship's location were possible. If a storm blew a ship off course or clouds hid the stars, it was impossible to know an exact location. These conditions made it difficult for sailors to travel long distances with any safety at all. Their search for new sea routes for trading and for starting new colonies was a dangerous occupation.

Not knowing where a ship was located could, and often did, prove to be deadly. A ship with a name familiar to all Americans, the *Mayflower*, had sailed from England for the coast of Virginia. The warm climate in Virginia would have given the settlers plenty of time to build shelters and to find food. Unfortunately, a storm blew the ship so far off course that it landed in Massachusetts, much farther north than Virginia. The results were disastrous; nearly half the Pilgrims died in the harsh cold of the first winter in their new home.

These navigational problems were being worked on by mathematicians and astronomers. In 1675, King Charles II established the position of Royal Astronomer. He named John Flamsteed to the post. Charles wanted to keep English shipowners and sailors from being "deprived of any help that the Heavens could supply, whereby Navigation could be made safer. . . ." Flamsteed was working on a new and more accurate catalog of Northern Hemisphere stars, since it was in that hemisphere that most of the mariners were found. He was also observing and recording the motions of the moon and the planets.

Edmond Halley became involved with navigation and its close connection with the heavens as he studied at St. Paul's School. He became a master of a branch of

18

This seventeenth century engraving (below) shows Flamsteed House in Greenwich Park, which was the old Royal Observatory. Designed by Christopher Wren and founded by King Charles II (left), the observatory was built in order to solve the problem of finding longitude at sea.

iew of the Observatory in Greenwich Park, belonging to the Kings Professor of Astronomy

mathematics called trigonometry that deals with the relationship of sides and angles of triangles. This knowledge is essential in both navigation and astronomy. While at St. Paul's, Edmond learned to use a celestial globe and to make a complete dial. A celestial globe is a model of the sky, just as a globe is a model of the earth. A dial is a type of navigational instrument used by seamen to help keep time accurately.

But it was in astronomy, the study of the stars, that Edmond found his true calling. He decided to devote his life to astronomy because, he said, it gave him such "pleasure as is impossible to explain to anyone who has not experienced it."

Edmond eventually became so familiar with the skies that a globe and mapmaker named Joseph Moxon said of him, "He studied the heavens so closely that if a star were displaced. . . he would presently find it out."

Step outside on a clear, dark night. Look up at the sky. With the many stars seen there, Moxon's statement about Edmond's familiarity with the sky is amazing.

Chapter 3

A TRAGIC LOSS AND A HAPPY GAIN

At the age of sixteen Edmond observed and measured the variation that exists between geographic north (the North Pole) and magnetic north, where a magnetic compass points. He noted various happenings in the sky ranging from what he called "a Blazing star" (which we would now call a nova) to eclipses of the sun. He knew of the Italian astronomer Galileo and his work using a telescope.

Also at sixteen, sadness entered Edmond's world. His mother died that year. No one knows now how or why she died. What is known is that she was buried in the fall of 1672 at a small town called Barking in Essex.

The next year, at seventeen, Edmond left St. Paul's School and went to Oxford University to enter Queen's College. Edmond's widowed father, as always encouraging his son, had several astronomical instruments made for Edmond to take to Oxford. These included a twenty-four-foot-long refractor telescope and a sextant two feet in diameter.

Example of a celestial globe dating from Halley's time

Edmond's fascination with and study of the heavens continued. Not long after arriving at Oxford, Edmond wrote a letter to the Royal Astronomer, John Flamsteed, about some observations he had made through his telescope. He asked Flamsteed courteously if he, Flamsteed, had observed "anything of like nature." Edmond had found some mistakes in the tables he was using to check planet positions.

Flamsteed was quite impressed with the letter and the self-confidence and determination Edmond showed in his observational abilities. Flamsteed and Halley began a correspondence and a friendship that continued for several years.

Chapter 4

SKY WATCHERS THROUGH THE CENTURIES

For thousands of years people have watched the skies. Both the Greeks and the Chinese, long before the birth of Christ, kept records of objects seen there. They gave names to groups of stars that reminded them of things they knew in their own lives: animals, people, birds. Most of the things they saw night after night became as familiar as old friends visiting with them.

Simply by watching the skies over a period of time, people knew that some objects did not appear to change positions, while other objects did. Eventually, because these events happened over and over again, like the twenty-eight-day repeating cycle of the moon, sky occurrences became less frightening and more explainable. The planets, however, had much more complicated movements. But eventually they, too, showed regular patterns that began to be recognized even though they could not be explained completely. It was still a comfort to know that everything was happening in an orderly way. As long as events happened as expected, all seemed right in the world.

Many of the ancient Greeks who studied the sky believed the earth was in the middle of all the activities they saw and recorded. In fact, they believed the earth was the center of the entire universe. They *knew* that the planets moved, but earth did not. They thought that the planets moved around the earth in circular paths.

The beliefs of the Greeks were handed down through the centuries until about the sixteenth century (1500 to 1599). Then a Polish astronomer named Nicholas Copernicus startled the world by saying that only the moon, and not the planets, moved in a circle around the earth. Furthermore, he said that the earth, just like all the other known planets, moved in a circle around the sun.

This idea was quite a new and different way of looking at the universe. While it helped account for some of the strange behavior of the planets, it brought with it a furor. Why, some said, that must mean that the earth was *not* the center of the universe, when everyone *knew* that it was! Others said it must mean that man was *not* the center of God's universe. This was a belief that could not be tolerated. Hundreds of years of believing in a certain idea could not be tossed aside so easily. Copernicus was not believed.

About one hundred years before Edmond Halley lived, a student from Denmark fought a duel in which a large piece of his nose was cut off. For the rest of his life, Tycho Brahe wore a false nose made of gold and silver. Tycho Brahe became a famous northern astronomer. He was one of the first to make careful observations and measurements of the heavens, adding to the growing knowledge about the sky. People all over the world were studying the sky and, bit by bit, some of the heavens' secrets were being unlocked. Knowledge brought understanding and understanding brought fewer fears about the unknown.

One of Tycho's students, a German named Johannes Kepler, had been studying the motions of planets. He thought that Copernicus was correct about the earth being one of the planets that moves around the sun. But he did not believe that the earth or the other planets moved in a circular path, or orbit, around the sun. He thought their orbits were more of an oval shape, rather than circular. This shape Kepler called an ellipse and he worked out the elliptical orbits for all the planets then known.

Kepler's theories of elliptical orbits for planets around the sun answered some more questions, but raised others. Why were the orbits elliptical rather than circular? Why did the planets seem to move faster as they got closer to the sun?

Tycho Brahe (1546-1601)   Johannes Kepler (1571-1630)

Chapter 5

THE ROYAL SOCIETY

The seventeenth century seems to mark the beginning of modern science. It was the time when the scientific method came into being. This method set down standards for everyone working in all fields of science. In the scientific method, a question is asked, information about the question is gathered, a possible solution is tried, a test is made, and some answers may be found. Perhaps what is found raises new questions and suggests further directions for other scientists to take. The entire process must be written down in such a way that other scientists can follow the same procedure and get the same results.

As each scientist found a small piece of the puzzle to explain the world around him, he told others about it. By this means more and more scientists knew what was being studied, what had been tried, and what questions were still unanswered. Scientists would meet whenever possible to talk about their current projects and problems. A favorite meeting place would be one of the new social gathering spots called coffeehouses. London had over five hundred coffeehouses. One was even built to float on the Thames River which runs through London.

But these face-to-face discussions were slow means of communicating what scientists were learning. It became obvious that there was a need for some kind of organization to gather all the information being discovered and get these findings out to others. Sparks from one mind might then kindle a new idea in another mind.

Some method of keeping scientists in touch was needed. Some things they were learning, like Copernicus's belief that the earth was not the center of the universe, were opposite to what religious leaders or the Church taught. It was not always wise to say aloud or put in writing what had been learned—some people had been burned at the stake for doing so.

Twelve Englishmen, interested in all the new discoveries being made, began meeting informally to talk about their work and experiments. These men included Isaac Newton, a mathematician; Robert Boyle, a chemist; Robert Hooke, a physicist; and Christopher Wren, a professor of astronomy and a mathematician (but better known today as an architect). They would not have called themselves "a physicist," "a chemist," or similar names. These divisions of science were created years later. They would probably have identified themselves as "natural scientists," men looking for solutions to the many down-to-earth problems of the day. They were the pioneers who discovered "natural laws." Their discoveries are the reason the seventeenth century is called the Century of Genius. What they learned made possible the Age of Invention in the eighteenth century (1700-1799).

One of these men, Robert Hooke, was a friend of King Charles II. Hooke called Charles's attention to the existence of this group of men, who referred to themselves as "The Invisible College." Charles took an immediate interest in the group. He granted them a charter in 1661 and gave them the name "The Royal Society of London for Improving Natural Knowledge," known more commonly today as "The Royal Society." This group has the distinction of being the world's oldest scientific society. Only those scientists who can meet the highest scientific standards are voted into the fellowship of the society; they become Fellows of the Royal Society. To have the letters "F.R.S." (Fellow of the Royal Society) after one's name is among the greatest honors any scientist can ever achieve, even today.

The Royal Society's goals were and still are to publish new scientific knowledge and promote its discussion while encouraging and promoting research.

Edmond Halley was very soon to take an active role in this society and continue working with it for many years.

Copy of Robert Hooke's compound microscope as described in his "Micrographia" in 1665

Chapter 6

SOUTH TO ST. HELENA

Edmond Halley was almost as interested in the every-day business of the world—things such as navigation and methods of building and the manufacturing of all kinds of things—as he was in the sky. Astronomy was a very practical science in Halley's time. Surveyors, chart and mapmakers, road and bridge builders, miners, sea captains—all had questions for which mathematicians and astronomers sought answers.

Edmond knew that John Flamsteed was working on accurate star charts at the new Greenwich Royal Observatory near London. So were Johannes Hevelius, an astronomer who lived and worked in Danzig, Poland, and J.D. Cassini, in Paris. All three men were preparing charts for a new catalog of the stars in the Northern Hemisphere (north of the equator). Each used slightly different methods in their observations.

Edmond decided he could do something useful which none of the other astronomers were doing. In fact, no one else had ever done what Edmond planned to do. He would make a chart of the stars in the Southern Hemisphere (south of the equator). If an accurate chart of those stars were available, most of the Southern Hemisphere would then be safe for navigation and commerce and exploration. The southern stars could not be seen in Europe and had never before been studied by an astronomer with good viewing instruments.

After researching where he could get the best viewing conditions of the southern skies, Halley decided on the tiny island of St. Helena. This island was a small way station for shipping used by an English trading company called the East India Company. It was later to be the place where France's emperor Napoleon was exiled to and died. Only forty-seven square miles in area, St. Helena had just a few houses. It shows as a dot on the globe in the Atlantic Ocean twelve hundred miles west of southern Africa.

At the age of nineteen, Edmond was so eager to begin his work that he left Queen's College before completing his degree and began making arrangements for his expedition. He received encouragement from King Charles II. He sought and received permission from the

Engrav'd for the Royal Magazine

The Island of S.t HELENA.
Belonging to the East India Company of England.

An eighteenth century engraving of the island of St. Helena. This island was a British possession. It was used as a watering place by ships from the East India Company. Edmond Halley came here to chart the southern skies.

East India Company to use their island for his project. They were interested enough in his work to give him free passage on one of their ships, the *Unity*. His father agreed to continue the three-hundred-pounds annual allowance he had been giving Edmond. In 1675, that was a large sum of money, especially considering that even the Royal Astronomer earned only one hundred pounds per year. Not only that, he had to pay an assistant's salary plus buy his own instruments!

A friend of Edmond, a Mr. Clerke, went along to be his assistant. Edmond took his two-foot quadrant and his twenty-four-foot refractor telescope, plus several smaller telescopes, a pendulum clock, and two micrometers, which are devices used for measuring very small distances or angles. Before he left London he also had a brass sextant with a 5½-inch radius made and fitted with telescopic sights to make his observations as accurate as possible.

After a three month voyage, the *Unity* arrived at St. Helena. Unfortunately, the excellent weather conditions that Edmond had hoped to find for observing did not happen. Rainstorms, clouds, and heavy fog made gathering the data he wanted very difficult. But every moment that it was possible to see the sky, Edmond studied it.

In spite of all his problems, Edmond still was able to record on his charts the positions of 341 stars, many of which had never before been shown on any star map. He found three bright stars that could not be seen in England. To pay honor to King Charles II for his help, Edmond named a new constellation *Robur Carolinum*, Latin for "Charles's Oak," after an event in the king's life.

Halley and Clerke worked for over a year before going back to London. There Edmond wrote his findings in a book with a 102-word title, but referred to as *The Catalog of the Southern Stars*. It was written in Latin, the scientific language of that time. It was the first study ever made of the southern stars based on actual telescopic observations rather than sightings by the naked eye.

In London, Edmond showed Robert Hooke, who was then the secretary of the Royal Society, the work he had done at St. Helena. Hooke, too, was very impressed by this young man, barely twenty-one years old, just as Flamsteed had been. Hooke took Edmond's star catalog and discussed it with the other Fellows of the Royal Society. They all agreed it was a very important effort.

Honors to young Halley began pouring in. King Charles II was delighted that a young English scientist had made an outstanding contribution in reducing navigation hazards and encouraging commerce. He wanted to honor Edmond as well. Knowing Edmond had left Oxford before he finished work on his degree, the king interceded on his behalf. Edmond received the degree of Master of Arts without having to meet the usual requirements.

Royal Astronomer John Flamsteed hailed Edmond's work and paid him a great compliment by calling him "the southern Tycho," after the famous northern astronomer Tycho Brahe.

Members of the Royal Society paid Edmond perhaps the greatest honor of all by electing him a Fellow of the Royal Society.

Edmond Halley was only twenty-two years old.

Chapter 7

EDMOND VISITS HEVELIUS

Edmond Halley enjoyed life. He had a quick mind and keen curiosity. People enjoyed being in his company. Even with his early success and the recognition that it brought, he did not change. In addition to his other gifts, he seemed to have the ability to get along with people who were not always easy to deal with. Flamsteed, for example, was at first a friend of Edmond, but later turned against him over some imagined slights. Halley never seemed to be jealous of the achievements of other scientists; in fact, he could and often did go out of his way to help them.

The ability to win people over worked for Edmond all his life. In 1679, soon after he was elected to the Royal Society, he visited the astronomer Johannes Hevelius in Danzig, Poland. Halley wanted to meet this famous man and to see his great observatory and instruments. Hevelius used instruments with open sights. English astronomers thought they did not give readings as accurate as their own instruments with cross-haired telescopic sights. (English telescopic sights were similar to rifle sights.) There had been many disagreements about which type of sight was best.

When Edmond went to Danzig, the old astronomer Hevelius was then in his sixties, but knew of Edmond's catalog of the southern stars. Edmond was met with great joy and respect by Hevelius and his wife, who acted as the old man's assistant. The young astronomer and the old astronomer went to Hevelius's observatory and began looking at the sky the very night Halley arrived.

Using both types of telescopes, they observed and made careful measurements of their observations. They found their figures were very similar; one type of telescope was not conclusively better than the other. Each continued to favor the kind of telescope he had been using.

Edmond stayed with Hevelius and his wife at their home for two months. Shortly after Edmond left, a fire destroyed Hevelius's observatory, library, home, his

Hevelius and his wife worked together using this sextant. One kept sight on a given star, the other person used the moving sight to line up with a second star whose angular distance from the given star was to be determined. From Johannes Hevelius, *Machina Coelestis*, Gedani (Danzig), 1673.

instruments, and nearly all of his belongings. It was never determined if the fire started because of arson or carelessness on the part of a coachman. Edmond helped Hevelius get new telescope lenses and other astronomical equipment to get his observatory working again.

Chapter 8

EDMOND MARRIES

For the next several years Edmond traveled to France and Italy to visit observatories and astronomers. In 1680 he saw a comet while traveling on the road between Calais and Paris in France. This sight, plus his usual strong curiosity, made him decide to investigate comets.

Two years later, after seeing the Great Comet of 1682 later to bear his name, he began reading everything he could about comets. That same year, Edmond married Mary Tooke, the daughter of a bank official. Mary was said to be an agreeable young gentlewoman and a person of real merit. They were wed in London and lived happily together for fifty-five years. They had one son. Just as Edmond had been named for his father, so he named his son Edmond, too. They became the parents of two daughters, Margaret and Katherine, as well.

Edmond and Mary's first home was in a suburb of London called Islington. He built a small observatory there, no doubt arousing the curiosity of his neighbors.

Edmond began making observations of the moon. The moon's movements were important to navigators. The moon tables printed then contained many errors that needed correcting.

Edmond's life was full and happy. He was doing the work he adored and he had a family he loved.

Then, in 1694, a tragedy occurred. His father was found dead under mysterious circumstances.

Some years after the death of Edmond's mother, Edmond's father had remarried. There is considerable evidence that this marriage was not a happy one; in fact, some have described it as disastrous. The elder Edmond left home one day and was never seen alive again. A young boy found his body in the river. It was never clearly established if Mr. Halley was murdered or committed suicide. Because his father had died without a will, Edmond had to put off the work he was doing to defend what little was remaining in his father's estate.

Chapter 9

ISAAC NEWTON

In 1684 Edmond was using geometry to try to prove the correctness of Johannes Kepler's theories about the motions of planets. He was unsuccessful. He was not able to prove his ideas mathematically in a way that other scientists could verify the work and find it acceptable. He discussed this problem with several Royal Society members and at length with two of them—Robert Hooke and Christopher Wren. Hooke claimed he had already worked out the proof that was needed. He promised to show his work to Halley and Wren. Wren told both Halley and Hooke that whoever could show the proof to him first would receive an expensive book Wren would buy.

Hooke never showed the others the proof he claimed he had.

Halley continued to work on finding an answer. His search led him to Isaac Newton, a brilliant mathematician working at Trinity College at Cambridge University.

Isaac Newton was very nearly the complete opposite of

Edmond Halley. He was fourteen years older than Edmond. He was not, as Edmond was, born into a well-to-do family. Isaac's family hoped he would follow in his father's occupation and become a farmer. Edmond's father doubtless had higher hopes for his boy than to become a soapboiler. Isaac's brilliance as a mathematician was not evident until one of his teachers at Cambridge recognized it. Edmond's father recognized his son's talents at an early age. Isaac was shy and withdrawn; Edmond was dynamic and outgoing. Isaac rarely shared the findings he made in his work. Edmond almost always did. Isaac's face is certainly well known now, appearing as it does on every British one-pound note. Edmond's face would be recognized by only a few people today.

During the Great Bubonic Plague of 1665, Cambridge University closed in an attempt to stop the spread of the plague. Isaac left Cambridge and went back to the family farm. There he experimented with light and telescope design, among other things. His experiments led him to advance the idea that white light is a mixture of light of all colors. He designed and built a telescope using a mirror in front of the lens, which greatly reduced the wobbles in the long-tube telescopes that astronomers used then. Reducing wobbles also reduced errors—a very important discovery indeed. Today this type of telescope is called a reflecting telescope and all large new telescopes are reflectors.

When the Royal Society learned of this new telescope design, Newton was asked to show a model to them. The Royal Society rewarded him by electing him a Fellow and then invited him to prepare a paper telling of other work he was doing. Newton later said he probably would not have written this paper on light and color without the Royal Society's invitation to do so. When it was published in the Royal Society's scientific journal (called the *Philosophical Transactions*), it brought a mixture of opinions. After this happened, poor, shy Newton became even more reluctant to tell anyone about his scientific activities. He would spend months, even years, making calculations, but would rarely bother to tell anyone of his findings.

In 1684, still puzzled over how to prove mathematically the motions planets make, Edmond went to Isaac Newton and talked to him about the problem. Newton told a delighted Edmond that he had worked out the solution sometime earlier. But when he began to look for his notes, Isaac could not find them. Edmond asked him if he would keep looking or work out the solution again. Isaac agreed. Not long after Edmond's visit, the notes Isaac prepared were sent to Edmond in London.

Because Edmond was a mathematician, too, he immediately knew something of great importance had been found. He realized that Isaac had developed an entirely new area of mathematics, later called calculus. Edmond excitedly hurried back to Cambridge. He and Isaac talked at great length about this mathematical proof, Isaac's notions of how the universe worked, and some other ideas Isaac had. Edmond realized how significant these ideas were and, using his powers of persuasion, got Isaac to agree to set his ideas down in book form. Edmond promised to ask the Royal Society for financial help in getting Newton's work published and into the hands of scientists the world over.

Edmond kept his promise and requested financial help from the Royal Society to pay for the publication of Newton's work. The Royal Society agreed to do so, but when it was time to take the book to the printer, the society lacked the needed funds. Edmond knew the value

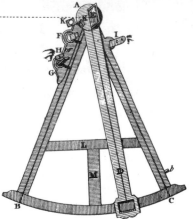

The Polish astronomer,
Nicholas Copernicus
(1473-1543), worked at
night in his rooftop observatory as shown above.
Halley used this mirror
quadrant or sextant (right)
in 1731.

Drawing of Tycho Brahe's great mural quadrant, showing the astronomer and the instruments he used in his work. Taken from *Astronomiae Instaurateae Mechanica*, 1598.

Jean Dominique Cassini (1625-1712) was director of the Paris Observatory shown in the background. From an engraving by Louis Cossin.

Flamsteed's equatorially mounted sextant (left) was fitted with a telescope: 1677. From John Flamsteed, *Historia Coelestis Britannica*, London, 1725.
Hevelius observed with a wooden-tubed, thirty foot, refracting telescope shown below. It had an inconvenient rope and block-and-tackle mounting. From Johannes Hevelius, *Selenographia*, Gdansk, 1647.

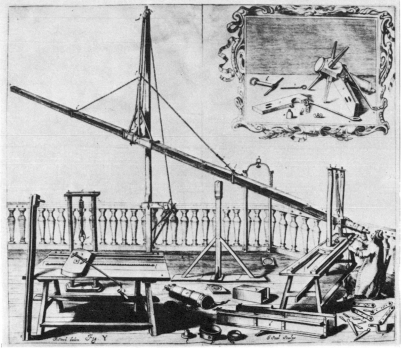

John Flamsteed
(1646-1719)
Engraving by Vertue taken
from the first volume of
Flamsteed's *Historia Coelestis Britannica*, London,
1725.

Christopher Wren
(1632-1723)
Engraving taken from a
portrait by Sir Godfrey
Kneller.

Johannes Hevelius
(1611-1687)

Robert Boyle, as a young
man, (1627-1691), taken
from Edmund Lodge, *Portraits of Illustrious Personages of Great Britain*, London, 1840.

This refracting telescope was fitted with quadrant and plumb bob so that the altitude of object observed could be noted. From Johannes Hevelius, *Selenographia*, Gedani (Gdansk/Danzig), 1647.

Oxford University

of Newton's work. He knew it had to be published. Putting aside his own work, he spent many months going over the printing. He paid all the expenses of publication out of his own pocket. Eventually sales of the work brought in enough money to repay Halley, but without his dedication to the task, the book might never have been printed.

The book was a monumental task. There were three separate parts. It took Newton nearly eighteen months to write it. Before publication of the last part of the book began, a problem surfaced. Robert Hooke claimed that some of Newton's ideas were really Hooke's ideas. Hooke wanted Newton to give him credit in the book. Edmond had to break this unwelcome news to Isaac. Hooke's claim angered Newton. It brought back reminders of the controversy his paper on light had caused. Newton threatened not to allow the last part of the book to be published. Edmond again had to use his persuasiveness. He was finally able to soothe Isaac. All three parts of the book were published in 1687.

Newton's book, written in Latin, was entitled *The Mathematical Principles of Natural Philosophy*, and is known simply as the *Principia*. It advanced Newton's idea that the force—which he called gravity—that makes an apple fall to the ground is the very same force working to keep the moon at an even distance from the earth and the earth and all the other planets moving on the same paths around the sun.

Edmond called the book "the divine treatise." His opinion has never been regarded as exaggerated. Some have even said it is the greatest work on natural science ever done by man. Its publication was one of those events that will forever stand as memorable in the history of science. It was not until Albert Einstein's time in the twentieth century that Newton's principles had to be changed even slightly. Newton showed that "heavenly bodies worked in one gigantic mathematical harmony," wrote Sir William C.D. Dampier, a scholar on the history of science.

Edmond Halley wrote a dedication entitled "Ode to Newton" in the *Principia*. This dedication, translated from the Latin by Leon Richardson, says:

"... now we know
the sharply veering ways
of comets, once

Isaac Newton (1642-1727)
From an engraving
after the portrait by
Vanderbank. From *The Gallery of Portraits,*
Vol. I, Charles Knight,
London, 1833.

A source of dread,
no longer do
we quail

Beneath appearances
of bearded
stars."

The *Principia* introduced Newton's theories on gravitation and the motions of planets. It gave the world new views of the universe. It was greeted with as much acclaim and represented as much of a scientific breakthrough as Edmond had believed it would.

No one can dispute the greatness of Isaac Newton, but without Edmond Halley, would the world ever have known of him?

Chapter 10

COMETS

Edmond served the Royal Society for fourteen years as corresponding clerk and later as secretary. His old headmaster from St. Paul's School, Thomas Gale, was a Fellow and they met again through the Royal Society. As corresponding clerk Edmond wrote letters to leading scientists all over the world, including Anton van Leeuwenhoek, one of the first to use the microscope. Edmond learned about many other discoveries. As these were reported to him, Edmond had them published in the Royal Society's journal so that others could share the new scientific knowledge.

During this time Edmond also continued his work on comets.

We now know that comets are fairly small celestial bodies moving about the sun in very long orbits. They have been described as chunks of "dirty ice" since they are thought to be made up of rock dust and ice. They usually consist of a central mass, called the nucleus or head, surrounded by a misty envelope (the coma) which extends into a stream (the tail) in the direction away from the sun. The tail is formed when the heat of the sun evaporates the ice. The gases that make up the ice are released, blowing dust particles away from the head of the comet.

In 1970 two comets were discovered to be surrounded by huge clouds of hydrogen gas.

Although there may be as many as 100 billion comets, fewer than 1,000 have been observed. Most comets exist in the cold outer fringes of the solar system. Most of what is known about comets has been discovered by scientists viewing them from earth at a distance of 3.5 million miles.

Long ago people spent much more time looking up at the sky than we do today. The word *comet* is from the Greek word meaning "the hairy one." People thought these strange objects looked like hairy or bearded stars. They were regarded with both fear and fascination. Familiar constellations and bright objects seen in the skies, even though they changed location throughout the year, gave people a sense of comfort as they noted the regularity of celestial events. But when something

Galileo demonstrated his telescope to the senate of Venice.

strange, like a comet, appeared, it was an extremely frightening occurrence. Comets seemed to come from out of nowhere and follow no regular order.

In an effort to explain them, people decided comets must be a sign that God was angry or that horrible things were about to happen. People believed that all sorts of awful things—assassinations, wars, floods, plagues, pestilence—were caused by comets. In 1456 the pope ordered the faithful to recite the Ave Maria three times daily and to pray for protection against the "devil and. . . the comet."

Although people did watch the sky, regular observation of celestial events to make computations and predictions was not common. Careful observation was done only when extraordinary happenings were taking place. No one knew what kind of paths comets made. Instruments were not very accurate and comets could be seen only for short periods of time. In 1577 Tycho Brahe had shown beyond doubt that comets were celestial objects that were very far away. Before then many people had believed that comets somehow rose up out of the atmosphere.

Ever since he had seen the 1680 comet, Edmond Halley had studied comets. After he and Isaac Newton discussed Newton's new ideas on gravitational attraction and the movements of heavenly objects, Halley tried to apply Newton's findings to his own calculations on comets. Edmond must have suspected that Newton's theories explained the strange behavior of comets from what he wrote in his "Ode to Newton" in the *Principia*. He studied all the records of earlier comet observations he could find. He calculated their orbits. At first he thought comets traveled in straight line paths. Edmond later decided comet paths were elliptical, as Kepler had said planets' orbits around the sun were. Because of Newton's discoveries of the gravitational attraction of large bodies on small bodies, Edmond realized that the planets would affect comet orbits. When he applied Newton's ideas to the study of the Great Comet of 1682 and of comets appearing in 1607, 1531, and 1456, he made a startling discovery. They all fit the same pattern!

Halley became convinced that it was not four different comets people on earth had seen, but the same comet returning four times—in a regular pattern!

By 1705 Halley believed that if he were correct in his findings, this same comet would appear again in 1758. He thought that it took about seventy-six years for this particular comet to make its orbit around the sun. The time could vary because of the effects of the gravitational attraction of the large planets Jupiter and Saturn. (Uranus, Neptune, and Pluto were all unknown at the time.) Halley was forty-nine years old in 1705. It was unlikely that he would live till 1758 and the age of one-hundred-and-two. In his published work predicting the comet's return, he asked that astronomers watch the skies carefully to acknowledge that an Englishman had predicted the return of the comet.

Halley's prediction was very bold. It was not greeted with a great amount of belief. But if the comet did return when Halley said it would, it would be a triumph both for Halley and for the principles of Isaac Newton.

In Halley's time there were no computers or adding machines. All computing had to be done by hand with pen and paper. A French mathematician, Alexis Clairant, and two assistants spent six months checking Halley's calculations. One of the assistants claimed the work was so exhausting that his health suffered ever after. The

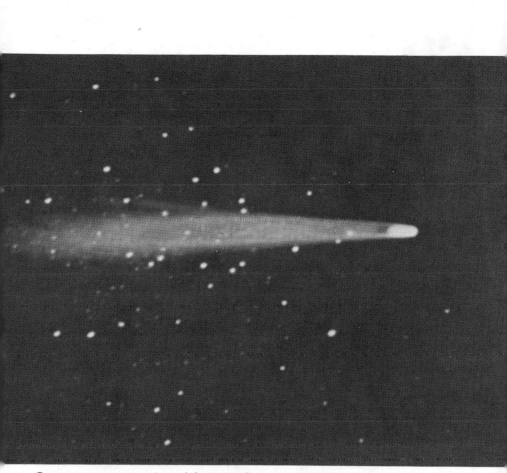

Computer reconstruction of the 1910 photograph of Halley's Comet

other assistant, a thirty-four-year-old woman described by Clairant as not pretty, but having "an elegant figure and a pretty little foot," seemed to have no long-lasting ill effects from the work. Their figures were in close agreement with Halley's own: only about a month's difference in the time the comet was to appear—a small difference in a period of seventy-six years' time!

Comets rarely behave exactly as predicted. Each time this comet returns, scientists are able to predict the date more precisely. After the 1758 return, predictions were within 5 days of its reappearance date in 1835 and only 2.7 days off schedule in 1910.

Halley, of course, did not live to see his prediction come true. As the date approached, Voltaire, a French philosopher, said that astronomers never went to bed in 1758 for fear of missing the comet. Amateur and professional astronomers alike searched the skies to have the honor of reporting the first sighting. Oddly enough, it was an amateur astronomer, Johann Georg Palitszch, a farmer living near Dresden, Germany, who first spotted it on a cold Christmas night in 1758 using a homemade seven-foot telescope. The sighting was an unprecedented triumph for Halley's prediction. It proved he was correct about comets. They are truly members of our solar system and they do have regular paths around the sun.

The sighting of the comet in 1758 marked, too, the establishment of the telescope as a powerful weapon of discovery, bringing in the age of modern astronomical observation.

To honor Edmond Halley for his remarkable prediction, the comet from that time has been called Halley's Comet. What he discovered about it removed much of the fear and superstition that had always surrounded the dreaded appearance of comets.

Chapter 11

SOME OTHER SCIENTIFIC CONTRIBUTIONS

In the twentieth century, nearly the only association made with the name "Halley" is "comet." The prediction of the return of the comet was, of course, a great achievement. But in Halley's lifetime it was only one of hundreds of items of practical information he contributed to the growing body of many branches of science.

At the Royal Society headquarters today in London, seventy-six of Halley's manuscripts may be seen, even though they are by no means the total of his work. The range of his interests becomes more apparent if one simply scans some of the studies he made. For example, he studied actions of tides and devised a theory that satisfied the facts of his observations, clearly showing the moon's effects on tides.

He studied springs, water vapor, rainbows, solar heating, monsoons, barometric pressure, magnetism, and gravity. He tried to explain the causes of trade winds and he is credited with developing the first meteorological chart. He worked on a method to keep large ships at sea in the wintertime without damage from ice. All of these things were of great importance, but especially so in the days of sailing ships.

He wrote about salt water evaporation. He thought that the age of the earth might be measured by the degree of saltiness of the oceans. He is regarded as the founder of scientific geophysics. In 1957, during the International Geophysical Year, the Royal Society named its permanent Antarctic scientific base Halley Bay to honor him.

Halley and Robert Hooke sometimes worked together. They measured cisterns in London. They also made observations of Jupiter through a telescope to record when the moon passed in front of Jupiter. It was, and still is, the best way to determine precisely the exact position of the moon. More practical information was added to the store of knowledge of a nation of seafaring people.

Halley was very interested in archaeology. He published a paper proving the time and place that Julius Caesar first landed in Britain, using evidence from records of an eclipse of the moon that took place at the time. Halley's union of archaeology with astronomy in this paper has only recently become known as archaeo-astronomy.

He studied the questions of the size of the universe and the number of stars it contained.

Most people in the early part of the eighteenth century believed the stars were fixed in one location and never moved. Halley proved that stars do move by using observations made fifteen hundred years earlier!

Using his own mathematical abilities and Newton's gravitational ideas in an effort to make guns more accurate, he calculated the pathway taken by bullets. He also studied the force of gunpowder and the resistance of air to projectiles.

Halley studied how long people live and devised a table of life expectancy. He demonstrated how these tables could be used by the insurance companies for calculating payments to people who lived longer than might be expected.

He was interested in the "art of living underwater." He wrote several papers about a diving bell he made and used. He described some of the difficulties of living underwater—what people inside a diving bell could sit on, what materials would be strong enough to stand the pressure, and why windows were needed so observers could look out. When he went underwater in the diving bell he made, he noticed that light coming in from under the bell was a pale green color, but light from the window was pale cherry red. When he cut his finger, he said the blood looked deep green and it seemed to bleed much more than it would have on the earth's surface. In these experiments, too, he learned about the painful pressure on the ears caused by depths and of the problems of changing often-breathed air. But Halley did manage to keep three men underwater sixty feet deep for nearly two hours "in perfect freedom as they had above." He worked on a method of walking underwater. He also designed a diving helmet and formed a company, hoping to manufacture and sell the helmet for use in salvaging ships wrecked at sea.

He translated geometry and astronomy books written in Arabic, a difficult language he may have learned from a professor of astronomy at Oxford.

It seems that almost nothing was too insignificant to escape Halley's notice. He wrote a paper that discussed ways to estimate how swift birds' wings must be to sus-

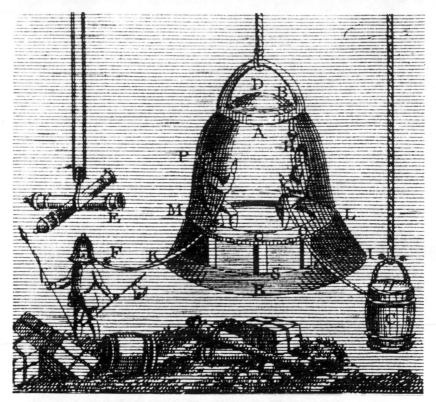

In Halley's diving bell two figures sit in the bell, and the air comes in through a tube from barrel (C, right). The figure outside the bell has a helmet with a breathing tube connected to the diving bell, but is otherwise free to move and work. Fresh barrels of air were sent down from a boat above. From W. Hooper, *Rational Recreations*, London, 1782.

Halley's chart of the trade winds and monsoons published in *Philosophical Transactions*

tain them in flying. Another paper theorized why, when houses are blown up with gunpowder, the windows of nearby houses fall outward into the street rather than inward.

In 1696 Halley and his family moved to Chester, England, 175 miles northwest of London. He was made deputy comptroller of the Royal Mint there and was to help supervise the making of new coins. During the years in Chester, he kept up his correspondence duties as clerk of the Royal Society and found time to continue his own scientific studies. He wrote an account of extraordinary hailstones which fell in Chester, and of an experiment he tried on Snowden Hill to measure the heights of mountains by using a barometer. He made more observations of moon eclipses and experimented with a method of measuring the earth's surface by using telescopic sights.

Halley was also interested in the human body. He wrote an observation on the dissection of a man by a Dr. Bernard, as well as another paper about a valve located near the eardrum.

Not only did medical science interest Halley, but so did medical oddities. He reported on a paper written by the doctor who attended a sixteen-year-old boy, Andrew

Rudloff, who was playing with a 16½-inch-long knife in his mouth and fell on it. The knife was forced down his throat and into his stomach. Surprisingly, the boy did not die. Nineteen months after the accident, the knife was removed from his stomach and was "exceedingly consumed in all dimensions" by the action of stomach acid on it.

Halley wrote many papers on shipping. When Peter the Great, the tsar (ruler) of Russia, visited Deptford, England, in 1696 to study British shipbuilding, he met with Halley several times. They talked about plans Peter had to establish a navy and to introduce science into Russia. The two of them got on well together and discussed many scientific and engineering concerns. Peter is given credit for modernizing Russia and making it into a world power.

Some modern writers have acknowledged Halley's brilliance and have then gone on to state that, in spite of it all, Halley believed the earth to be hollow. Not only did he think the earth was hollow, but he also believed that "some sort of weird life might exist deep within it."

In England in the seventeenth century, there were several upheavals over religious beliefs. Halley was an independent thinker on religious questions. He had a lively sense of humor and did not mind teasing his fellow scientists about their religious beliefs. Few doubted Halley believed in God, but he did not consider every word in the Bible to be literally true. He believed, for example, that the Great Flood (or "deluge" as Halley called it) might have been caused by some phenomenon, perhaps a giant comet. Because he held a belief that was not the official view of the Church of England, Halley was accused of heresy, a very serious charge in those days.

Halley once had hoped to get an appointment as a professor at Oxford. In his day professors were questioned by church officials on their beliefs. Halley eventually got a professorship, but his beliefs caused a delay in the appointment.

Chapter 12

HALLEY'S LATER YEARS

In 1698, at the age of forty-two, Halley was called on by King William and Queen Mary to find out why compasses at different places on the ocean varied in their readings from true north. He was also asked to visit English settlements in North America to determine their correct latitude and longitude. He was to try to discover what lands lay to the south of the Atlantic Ocean as well.

The voyage was to be the first scientific expedition carried out under the direction of the British crown. The king and queen gave him naval command of a small vessel called a pink and named the *Paramore*. The pink had a high poop deck and wide sides giving excellent storage space. Since the voyage was to last about a year, storage space was essential for its crew of twenty.

Although Halley was well acquainted with navigation, he had never been in charge of a ship at sea. His second in command, a lieutenant named Harrison, made the insulting remark, in front of the crew, that Halley had no sea skills and "wasn't fit to manage a long boat." Halley's nature was usually easygoing, but this remark and other insubordinations by Harrison could not be overlooked. He put the man under arrest and sailed back to England where he had the lieutenant court-martialed.

In the fall of 1699, with a new lieutenant, Halley sailed the *Paramore* south until it met with some icebergs. Then he sailed north, back to the island of St. Helena. Mountains of ice, fog, and foul weather made this leg of the voyage quite dangerous. From St. Helena he sailed to Brazil, then to the Barbados, and then on to the coast of North America and finally back to England. During the voyage the *Paramore* crossed the equator four times. Halley was able to observe compass variations as well as the behavior of pendulum clocks near the equator. With his long telescope he watched several eclipses.

As soon as he got back to England, Halley used what he learned during the long voyage to publish a new and valuable chart for England's seamen.

Halley was proud of this work, but perhaps he was proudest of the fact that, in spite of having no previous seafaring experience, he had sailed thousands of miles and had brought back the ship and the men on board safely.

During the three years that Halley commanded the pink, he suggested chart corrections to the British Admiralty on the waters around England. He determined the correct position of the Scilly Islands, off the southwestern coast of England, and he continued his study of the tides and currents through the English Channel. All his findings increased the safety of ships sailing these waters.

For a short time he acted as a technical adviser to Queen Anne when she sent him to Europe to check on harbor fortifications and to survey ports during the War of Spanish Succession.

Two years after his last expedition, he was appointed a professor of geometry at Oxford and was further honored with the degree of Doctor of Laws.

His work with the Royal Society continued and, in 1713, he was made secretary to the Royal Society, a post he held for eight years.

Chapter 13

ROYAL ASTRONOMER

In 1719, John Flamsteed died. Dr. Edmond Halley was the obvious choice as second Royal Astronomer. The appointment may have been the first time there was complete public recognition of Halley's work.

Edmond and Mary moved to Greenwich to the Royal Observatory. He managed to get 500 pounds from the government to buy new equipment for the observatory. Flamsteed's widow had taken all the instruments since her husband had paid for them from his wages.

Edmond was still greatly interested in navigational problems in his position as Royal Astronomer. Because he believed that the key needed to find longitude at sea was the positions of the moon, Halley continued to study the moon's movements and positions on different dates and in different phases of its cycle. Flamsteed had started this enormous work, but had not completed it. Halley spent the next eighteen years working to improve lunar tables and eventually, at the age of eighty-two, finished the work. Perhaps because of his age, or because of the equipment he used, Halley did not take the great care needed in making the proper adjustments to his equipment. His observations, however, were still of value to navigators and were improvements over what had been available to them previously.

But Edmond Halley was aging. Few men lived beyond the age of fifty in the 1700s. By the time he reached his eighth decade, he was in declining health. Mary, his wife, died in 1736. The next year he suffered a small stroke and his right hand was affected by slight paralysis. He had rarely been ill in his long life, but by the age of eighty-three his health seemed to go down rapidly. He ate almost nothing but fish, one of his friends wrote, because he had no teeth. People who visited him said that even though his body's powers were failing quickly, his memory and cheerfulness remained unimpaired.

His only son, Edmond, who was a surgeon, died in 1741.

Finally, in 1742, at the age of eighty-six, Edmond Halley died while sitting in his chair. He was buried beside his beloved wife in the churchyard of Lee in Kent, near the Royal Observatory.

Engraving of Edmond Halley taken from the portrait by Richard Phillips painted about 1720, soon after Halley became Royal Astronomer. From *The Biographical Magazine*, London, 1794.

Chapter 14

HALLEY REMEMBERED

Many honors had come to Edmond Halley during his lifetime; others came long after his death. During the time he lived he was regarded as a genius. Years later it became a bit easier to look back and put in perspective what he had accomplished over the eighty-six years of his life.

Astronomer Joseph Lalande called Halley "a charming man of rare intelligence" and "the greatest of English astronomers. . . ranking next to Newton among the scientific Englishmen of his time."

English professor and Halley biographer E.F. Mac-Pike says that three things are especially noticeable about Halley: he was extremely energetic and managed to do an enormous amount of work during his eighty-six years; he was jovial and good-natured and admired and applauded other people's work; and he worked on problems that were of great practical use.

Colin A. Ronan has also studied and written about Edmond Halley. He calls Halley one of the most brilliant and respected scientists of the late seventeenth and early eighteenth centuries. He was the first to apply Newton's theories and to confirm Newton's genius, Ronan says. Halley also made great contributions toward improving scientific instruments. Halley's findings and his work on comets form the basis of the scientific study done on comets yet today. Mr. Ronan ends by saying that the world of science is "permanently in his debt."

Edmond Halley was mainly an astronomer. His work in that field, and all others he excelled in, made him useful both to his country and to the entire world. Today we could also call him a meteorologist, a physicist, an archaeologist, an oceanographer, a geographer, a navigator, an engineer, a geologist, an inventor, and even a social statistician because of the contributions he made in all those areas of science. His life was filled with curiosity, excitement, and the thrill of discovery. His breed was and is very rare.

As one person said, "The world is less likely to see another Halley than another Newton." There is little doubt that Edmond Halley was one of the greatest men of science who ever lived.

CAROLO II. D.G. MAG. BRIT. FRAN. & HIB. REGI SEMPER AUG.

Hanc AUSTRALIS HEMISPHÆRII tabulam
Nuperis obfervationibus juffu Regio fufceptis, reftitutam.
Plurimifq stellis nondum Globo afcriptis locupletatam.
submifse offert

Subditus Humillimus EDMUNDUS HALLEIUS e Coll: Reg: Oxon:

Halley's planisphere of the southern stars (by kind permission of Sir
Edward Bullard)

SUGGESTIONS FOR ACTIVE INVOLVEMENT

Edmond Halley was a remarkable scientist. He would have been remarkable no matter when he lived. Is it possible to have an Edmond Halley today? Scientists are more numerous; more scientific advances have been made; communication is much faster and easier. Yet it seems unlikely that one person could ever accomplish again all the things that Halley did in his lifetime. Science today generally takes place in government-sponsored programs or in think tanks. Debate whether or not a scientist today could emerge in the mold of Edmond Halley or any of the other scientists mentioned in this book.

* * * * * * * *

King Charles II seems to have been a remarkable monarch for many reasons, but especially because of his interest in finding solutions to the practical problems of his country. He reigned from 1660 to 1685 and was probably the last English monarch to have a complete set of armor made. What other achievements besides chartering the Royal Society and helping Halley did he accomplish?

Many astronomers have studied comets. Read about some of them. Find out about the "comet ferret" Charles Messier, a French astronomer, who discovered at least fifteen comets. Maria Mitchell was an American astronomer who also discovered comets. She was the first (and until 1943, the only) woman elected to the American Academy of Arts and Sciences in Boston. Read more about this brilliant teacher and scientist.

* * * * * * * * *

Johann Georg Palitszch, an amateur astronomer, beat the pros in 1758 in spotting the return of Halley's Comet. Many comets have been found by amateur astronomers—some of whom have been teenagers. Amateurs can look for comets for fun, while professional astronomers cannot use their time hunting for comets. Report on some of the comets first sighted by amateurs.

If you are looking for comets and believe you have spotted one, notify the International Astronomical Union in Cambridge, Massachusetts, to report your finding. Remember, the discoverer of a new comet has the honor of having it named after him or her.

Each time a comet goes around the sun, material from the nucleus is vaporized to make the tail. In theory, then, the comet ought to be growing smaller and eventually cease to exist. Is there any evidence that Halley's Comet is becoming smaller?

* * * * * * * *

Even today people over the world are frightened by events that they do not understand, such as comets. Many people who were youngsters during Halley's Comet's last visit in 1910 are still living. Ask some of them to share their thoughts and feelings or memories about the comet. Some will have delightful stories and others will recall it as a time filled with the fear that the world was ending and all on earth would die as the earth passed through the comet's tail.

* * * * * * * *

In the 1950s, a Dutch astronomer named Oort said he thought comets are probably formed in the freezing darkness beyond Jupiter and perhaps even beyond Pluto, where they spend most of their lives. Comets contain what may be the oldest, most primitive unchanged original materials in our solar system. If scientists could study some of a comet's material, it might give clues to the origin of our solar system.

To get such clues, the National Aeronautics and Space Administration (NASA) wanted to send a space probe to fly by Halley's Comet when it is near us to gather some of its material. Unfortunately the project had to be abandoned because of time and cost. Several other countries are still planning some kind of space encounter. Research their ideas of how they will accomplish this. Report your findings.

* * * * * * * *

Some scientists have studied the effect of our nine planets' gravity on Halley's Comet and its orbit. They do not believe that the gravitational pull of the planets is enough to account for why some trips of the comet take more time than others. They reason that the variation might be due to the existence of a yet-undiscovered tenth planet in our solar system. One scientist predicts that this planet, when found, will be three times Saturn's size and will take five hundred years to go around the sun! Are there any other theories about the possible existence of an unknown tenth planet? Did scientists make predictions like this before the discovery of any of the other planets?

Could it be possible that some of the moons of other planets are really comets that have become caught in strong planetary gravitational pull?

* * * * * * * *

The International Halley Watch has been organized to coordinate by measurement and photographs the activities of about thirty observatories and many interested observers worldwide. It is hoped that this network will allow Halley's Comet to be seen at any hour of the day or night. Donald K. Yeomans of the Jet Propulsion Laboratory in Pasadena, California, has written about the International Halley Watch. Find some of his articles or books and report on the watch.

* * * * * * * *

Outdoor lighting in the United States has increased tremendously in recent years. So much light now brightens the nighttime sky that by 1986 perhaps the only people who can see Halley's Comet are those who live in remote areas. The Light Pollution Committee of the Astronomical League is trying to get towns and cities to dim their lights for a short time when the comet passes. What are some of the actions you as an individual or groups of people might take in your town or city to lessen light pollution?

Contact Jerry M. Sherlin, chairman, Astronomical League Committee on Light Pollution, Box 1842, Alamagordo, New Mexico 88310 for information on what this group is doing.

* * * * * * * * *

Earthlings speculate on the sight of Halley's Comet. Imagine *you* are Halley's Comet. What would your description be of what you see of earth? Who or what might live there? Or could it be lived on?

* * * * * * * * *

Larger libraries have microfilms of newspapers dating from 1910 and before. Look at some of these microfilms and re-create, briefly, America in 1910. Who was president? What were some of the major issues being discussed? What were the "facts" or stories being circulated about Halley's Comet? Were we at war? Did any major disasters occur that were blamed on the comet? What were some of the odd or humorous happenings you read about?

Very sophisticated instruments have been developed since we entered the so-called space age in the 1950s. Radio telescopes, infrared telescopes, wide-angle telescopes—all represent tremendous advances in the study of astronomy. Research and discuss how these instruments may be used to add to our knowledge of comets.

* * * * * * * *

Plan to collect the memorabilia that will be produced in quantity during Halley's Comet's return. Posters, medals, helmets, glass items, even comet pills were sold in 1910. Design something you might make millions of dollars of profit on to commemorate Halley's Comet.

* * * * * * * *

This vertical sundial on the Market Hall, in Warwick, England dates from 1620.

CHRONOLOGY OF HALLEY'S LIFE

Year	Age	Event
1656		Born in London, England.
1659	3	Charles II restored to throne. Bubonic plague in England.
1665	9	Father's apprentice teaches him writing and "arithmetique."
1666	10	Great London Fire.
1671	15	At St. Paul's School; appointed captain.
1672	16	Mother dies. Measures magnetic compass variations at St. Paul's. Decides to devote life to astronomy.
1673	17	Enters Queen's College, Oxford.
1674	18	Writes to John Flamsteed, Royal Astronomer.
1675	19	At St. Helena, observing southern skies.
1676	20	Writes *The Catalog of the Southern Stars*; publishes first scientific paper on planetary motion.
1677	21	Granted Oxford degree.
1678	22	Elected Fellow of the Royal Society. Visits Hevelius in Danzig, Poland.

1680	24	Tours France and Italy. Sees comet of 1680. Begins investigation of comets.
1682	26	Marries Mary Tooke. Establishes home and small observatory at Islington. Sees comet of 1682.
1684	28	Consults with Issac Newton. Father Edmond Halley dies under mysterious circumstances.
1685	29	Appointed clerk of the Royal Society.
1688	32	Two daughters, Katherine and Margaret, born.
1691	35	Refused chair at Oxford. Publishes paper linking archaeology and astronomy on Caesar's landing in England.
1692-96	36-40	Designs diving bell and helmet, forming company to sell them. Becomes deputy comptroller of mint at Chester in 1696.
1698	42	Peter the Great of Russia visits England and consults with Halley. Commissioned and working on the *Paramore*.
1701-02	45-46	Technical adviser to Queen Anne in War of Spanish Succession. Checking on harbor fortifications and surveying ports. Last expedition; checks English Channel.

1704	48	Appointed Savilian professor of geometry at Oxford; honored with degree of Doctor of Laws.
1705	49	Makes prediction that Great Comet of 1682 will return in 1758.
1713-21	57-65	Secretary to the Royal Society.
1714	58	Calculates exact position of track of shadow of the total solar eclipse due in 1715.
1716	60	Records ideas and experiences of living underwater.
1720	64	Appointed Royal Astronomer, succeeding John Flamsteed.
1729	73	Elected a Foreign Member of the *Academie des Sciences.*
1732-33	76-77	Last papers published.
1736	80	Mary, his wife, dies. Halley makes his will; has small stroke.
1737	81	Right hand affected by paralysis; in declining health.
1739	83	Bodily powers rapidly failing.
1741	85	Son Edmond Halley dies.
1742	86	Edmond Halley dies.

STAGE-TO-STAGE FOLLOWING HALLEY'S COMET

(Based on information from Donald K. Yeomans, Jet Propulsion Lab, Pasadena, California, and *Scientific American* magazine.)

During November, 1985   Halley's Comet passes earth on its way to the sun. It is invisible to the naked eye. This may be the best observing period for the Northern Hemisphere.

End of December, 1985   Halley's Comet may be visible using a good pair of binoculars after sunset.

Third week of January, 1986   The comet may be visible to the naked eye low on the western horizon after sunset, but no brighter than a relatively faint star. The comet will pass beyond the sun, a little to the north of it, and will be invisible in the bright sunlight. Once on the other side, Halley's Comet will be visible to the naked eye an hour before sunrise. After that, it will rise earlier each day, while heading away toward the south.

February 9, 1986   Halley's Comet reaches perihelion, or its closest point to the sun. It will be hard to see because the comet and earth are essentially on opposite sides of the sun.

March 7, 1986	Halley's Comet will almost be in line with the moon.
April, 1986	This is the prime observing period in the Southern Hemisphere.
April 11, 1986	Halley's Comet will be at its closest point to earth, high overhead in Australia, New Zealand, and Argentina in the constellation of Lupus and relatively bright. It will be low on the southern horizon in the United States and the Mediterranean area and invisible in northern Europe.
Last few days of April, 1986	Creeping northward slowly, the comet may be seen as an evening sky object, but growing fainter. This time period may be the best view the Southern Hemisphere will have.
Early May, 1986	As the earth comes close to Halley's orbit, there will be a meteor shower seven weeks after the comet itself has passed the spot. To see the comet itself will require powerful binoculars or a small telescope.

BIBLIOGRAPHY

Books

Anderson, Norman D., and Brown, Walter R. *Halley's Comet*. New York: Dodd, Mead and Company, 1981.

Armitage, Angus. *Edmond Halley*. London: Nelson, 1966.

Ash, Russell, and Grant, Ian. *Comets: Earth's Most Mysterious Visitors from Space*. New York: Bounty Books, a division of Crown Publishers, Inc., 1973.

Asimov, Isaac. *How Did We Find Out About Comets?* New York: Walker and Co., 1975.

Bailey, Francis. *Memoirs of the Royal Astronomical Society*. London: Royal Astronomical Society, 1843.

Branley, Franklyn M. *Comets, Meteoroids, and Asteroids: Mavericks of the Solar System*. New York: Thomas Y. Crowell Co., 1974.

Brown, Peter Lancaster. *Comets, Meteorites and Men*. New York: Taplinger Publishing Co., 1973.

Calder, Nigel. *The Comet Is Coming!* New York: Viking Press, 1980.

Daiches, Davis, and Flower, John. *Literary Landscapes of the British Isles*. London: Paddington Press, 1979.

Freeman, Mae and Ira. *Fun With Astronomy*. New York: Random House, 1953.

French, Bevan M., and Maran, Stephen P., eds. *A Meeting With the Universe*. Washington, D.C.: National Aeronautics and Space Administration, 1981.

Hartley, Dorothy. *Lost Country Life*. New York: Pantheon, 1980.

Heuer, Kenneth. *Wonders of the Heavens*. New York: Dodd, Mead and Co., 1954.

MacPike, Eugene Fairfield. *Correspondence and Papers of Edmond Halley*. Oxford: Clarendon Press, 1932.

———. *Dr. Edmond Halley: A Bibliographical Guide to His Life and Work Arranged Chronologically*. London: Taylor & Francis, Ltd., 1939.

————. *Edmond Halley: The Man*. London: Taylor & Francis, no date.

Muirden, James. *The Amateur Astronomer's Handbook: A Guide to Exploring the Heavens*. New York: Thomas Y. Crowell, 1968.

Page, Thornton, and Page, Lou Williams. eds. *Neighbors of the Earth: Planets, Comets, and the Debris of Space*. New York: The Macmillan Company, 1965.

Pooley, Robert C. et al. *England in Literature*. Chicago: Scott, Foresman and Company, 1963.

Richardson, Robert S. *Getting Acquainted With Comets*. New York: McGraw-Hill, 1967.

Ronan, Colin A. *Astronomers Royal*. New York: Doubleday and Co., 1969.

————. *Edmond Halley: Genius in Eclipse*. New York: Doubleday and Co., 1969.

The Royal Society. *The Royal Society: A Brief Guide to Its Activities*. London: The Royal Society, January, 1981.

————. *The Royal Society's Portraits and Busts*. London: The Royal Society of London, February, 1981.

Sarnoff, Jane, and Ruffins, Reynold. *Space: A Fact and Riddle Book*. New York: Charles Scribner's Sons, 1978.

Stephen and Lee, eds. *Dictionary of National Biography*. Vol. 8. Oxford: University Press, 1968.

Williams-Ellis, Amabel. *Courageous Lives: Stories of Nine Good Citizens*. New York: Coward-McCann, Inc., 1939.

———— and Fisher, F.J. *The Story of English Life*. New York: Coward-McCann, Inc., 1936.

Wyler, Rose, and Ames, Gerald. *The Golden Book of Astronomy*. New York: Golden Press (Simon & Schuster, Inc.), 1955.

Yeomans, Donald K. *The Comet Halley Handbook: An Observer's Guide*. Created for the International Halley Watch, January 15, 1981.

Periodicals

Asimov, Isaac. "Why Do Comets Have Tails?" *Science Digest*, August, 1971.

Bates, Ralph S. "Second Astronomer Royal, Edmond Halley." *Sky and Telescope*, March, 1942.

Beck, Joan. "Modern Man Blinded to Superstar's Fly By." *Dayton Daily News*, May 16, 1982.

Biddy, Francis C. "Comet Watcher's Big Chance." *Instructor*, January, 1974.

"The Comets Did It." *Time*, September 6, 1977.

"Comets: Readings from Scientific American." *Scientific American*, 1981.

"The Coming of Halley: The World Readies." *Science News*, March 15, 1980.

Covault, Craig. "NASA Plans New Space Missions." *Avaition Week & Space Technology*, April 17, 1978.

"Edmond Halley at St. Helena." *Sky and Telescope*, August, 1970.

Etz, Donald V. "Comets in the Bible." *Christianity Today*, December 21, 1973.

Franklin, Kenneth L. "Here Comes the Heavens' Most Notorious 'Dirty Snowball'." *Science Digest*, April, 1980.

Gingerich, Owen. "Tycho Brahe and the Great Comet of 1577." *Sky and Telescope*, December, 1977.

"Halley's Comet." *Sky and Telescope*, November, 1977.

"Halley's Comet and a Hypothetical New Planet." *Sky and Telescope*, November, 1972.

"Halley's Comet: Don't Expect Too Much." *Science News*, June 7, 1975.

Howse, Derek. "Restoration at Greenwich Observatory." *Sky and Telescope*, July, 1970.

"In Quest of Halley's Comet." *Science*, May 7, 1982.

Jungquist, Hazel. "A Dreaded Visitor." *Instructor*, January, 1974.

MacPike, E.F. "Dr. Edmond Halley's Marriage and Children." *The Genealogical Quarterly*, September, 1935.

Maran, Stephen P. "Getting Ready for Halley." *Natural History*, November, 1981.

Olson, Roberta J.M. "Giotto's Portrait of Halley's Comet." *Scientific American*, May, 1979.

Oppenheimer, Michael, and Haimson, Leonie. "The Comet Syndrome." *Natural History*, December, 1980.

"Prediction." *Sky and Telescope*, June, 1975.

"Probing Comets." *USA Today*, December, 1980.

Ronan, Colin A. "Halley, Edmond." *Dictionary of Scientific Biography*. Vol. 6. New York: Charles Scribner's Sons, 1962.

Roosen, Robert G., and Marsden, Brian G. "Observing Prospects for Halley's Comet." *Sky and Telescope*, November, 1977.

Rosen, Edward. "Brahe, Tycho." *World Book Encyclopedia*. Vol. 2. Chicago: Field Enterprises Educational Corp., 1974.

Stough, Charles. "Newsletter." *Dayton Daily News*, June 14, 1982.

Valentry, Duane. "The Worst of Halley's Comet." *Modern Maturity*, April-May, 1982.

Washburn, Mark. "In Pursuit of Halley's Comet." *Sky and Telescope*, February, 1981.

Weaver, Kenneth F. "Giant Comet Grazes the Sun." *National Geographic*, February, 1966.

———. "How to Catch a Passing Comet." *National Geographic*, January, 1974.

Whipple, Fred L. "The Spin of Comets." *Scientific American*, March, 1980.

GLOSSARY

ALGEBRA - a branch of mathematics in which the relationships and properties of numbers are expressed and analyzed in terms of letters, numerals, and abstract symbols.

ARCHAEOLOGY - scientific study of the human past through excavation or examination of such physical remains as tools, artifacts, or architecture.

ASTRONOMY - the science that deals with the planets, stars, and other heavenly bodies, including a study of their physical characteristics, relative positions, and motions.

BAROMETER - an instrument for measuring atmospheric pressure, used in weather forecasting and to determine height above sea level.

BLACK DEATH - epidemic of bubonic plague that spread through Europe, Africa, and Asia in the fourteenth century and in England in the seventeenth century.

BUBONIC PLAGUE - a serious disease carried to humans by fleas from infected rodents.

CALCULUS - any method or system of calculations in higher mathematics, using a special system of algebraic notation.

CELESTIAL - of or relating to the sky or heavens.

CISTERN - a reservoir for storing liquids, especially rainwater.

CIVIL WAR - a war between two sections or groups within a country.

COMMERCE - business transactions involving the exchange or purchase and sale of commodities or services, especially on a large scale.

COMPASS - an instrument for determining and showing directions, consisting of a magnetized needle which is freely suspended on a pivot and points to the north magnetic pole.

COMPUTATION - the act, process, or method of computing.

CONSTELLATIONS - any of eighty-eight groups of stars, many of which traditionally represent characters and objects in ancient mythology.

CORRESPONDING CLERK - one who exchanges or handles written correspondence.

COURT-MARTIAL - a military court that tries persons subject to military law.

CYCLE - complete course or series of events or phenomena that recur regularly in a definite sequence.

DECADE - a period of ten years.

DEGREE - a rank or title given by an academic institution for completion of a course of study or as an honorary distinction.

DIAL - a graduated surface on which the amount or degree of something is indicated by a moving pointer or index, as the face of a clock, compass, meter, or gauge.

DIPLOMATIC - possessing or exhibiting skill or tact in dealing with other people.

DISSECT - to cut apart or divide into parts for the purpose of study or scientific examination.

DIVING BELL - a large, hollow watertight container open at the bottom and filled with compressed air, used for work underwater.

ECLIPSE - apparent partial or total darkening of one celestial body by its passage through the shadow of another. In a solar eclipse the moon passes between the earth and the sun; in a lunar eclipse the earth moves between the sun and the moon.

ELLIPSE - a flattened or stretched out circle.

ELLIPTICAL - related to or shaped like an ellipse.

EQUATOR - the imaginary line circling the earth halfway between the north and south poles and from which degrees of latitude are measured.

ESTATE - property or possessions; everything owned by one person at the time of death or on becoming bankrupt.

EVAPORATE - to be changed from a liquid or solid into a gas; to give off moisture.

EXECUTE - to put to death in accordance with a legal sentence.

EXILED - expelled or voluntarily absent from one's country or home.

FOUL - extremely offensive to the senses, especially the sense of smell.

FUROR - frenzy or rage.

GASES - forms of matter, as distinguished from solids or liquids.

GENERATE - to produce or cause to be.

GEOGRAPHER - an expert in or student of geography.

GEOMETRY - branch of mathematics that deals with properties, measurements, and relations of points, lines, angles, plane figures, and solids.

GEOPHYSICS - branch of earth science dealing with the physical nature, motions, atmosphere, and hydrosphere of the earth. It includes seismology, oceanography, meteorology, and geodesy.

GRAVITATION - the force of mutual attraction that exists between any two bodies in the universe.

GRAVITY - gravitational force that the earth exerts on bodies at or near its surface. The pull of gravity on a body is called the weight of the body.

HEMISPHERE - one half of the earth, as divided by the equator or the Greenwich meridian. The equator divides the earth into the Northern and Southern Hemispheres; the Greenwich meridian divides it into the Eastern and Western Hemispheres.

HERESY - religious belief or doctrine that is at variance with accepted church doctrine.

HYDROGEN - nonmetallic element that is a highly flammable gas at normal temperatures.

INSUBORDINATE - disobedient; disrespectful of authority.

INTERCEDE - to plead on behalf of another or others.

JOVIAL - characterized by hearty, good-natured humor.

LATITUDE - the distance north or south of the equator expressed as degrees measured from the earth's center.

LONGITUDE - distance on the earth's surface measured in degrees east and west of the prime meridian and expressed by imaginary lines.

MAGNETIC NORTH - direction toward which the north-seeking end of a compass needle points, usually differing from true geographic north.

MASS - a coherent body of matter having an indefinite shape and a relatively large size.

MASTER OF ARTS - a master's degree granted by a college or university to a person who had completed an advanced course of study.

MATHEMATICIAN - one who is an expert in or a student of mathematics.

METEOROLOGIST - the scientist who studies meteorology, the atmosphere and the changes that take place within it; an important branch of meteorology is the study of weather.

MINT - a place where money is coined by authority of the government.

MORTALITY TABLE - a table that predicts the number of deaths in a given time or place.

NATURAL SCIENCE - any or all of the sciences concerned with the physical universe, including biology, chemistry, and geology.

NAVIGATION - art or science of determining and directing the position and course of ships and aircraft.

NOVA - a star that rapidly increases in brightness and then gradually fades to its original magnitude.

OBSERVATIONS - making examinations, noting and recording facts or phenomena especially for scientific study.

OCCULTATION - eclipse of one celestial body by the passing of another between it and the observer.

ODDITIES - things that are odd or peculiar.

ONE-POUND NOTE - basic paper money unit of England.

PARALYSIS - loss of powers of motion or sensation in a muscle due to a disease or injury to the nervous system.

PESTILENCE - any highly infectious, epidemic disease, especially bubonic plague.

PHASES - states or stages of development of a person or thing.

PHENOMENA - facts, events, or conditions that can be perceived by the senses.

PHILOSOPHER - one who studies or is an expert in philosophy.

PHYSICIST - one who is a student of or expert in physics.

PREDICT - to announce or declare something is going to happen before the actual event.

PROJECTILE - object that is designed to be shot or otherwise projected, as a bullet.

QUADRANT - quarter of a circle. Also, instrument used in navigation and astronomy for measuring altitude or angular distances above the horizon.

REFRACTOR - a telescope that refracts (breaks up) light to form an image.

RESEARCH - systematic study or investigation in a particular field, usually as a basis for new facts or interpretations.

ROYAL ASTRONOMER - the astronomer appointed by the crown.

ROYAL OBSERVATORY - a building designed for making scientific observations.

SALINE - consisting of or containing salt.

SALVAGING - saving a ship or its crew or cargo from loss or destruction.

SCHOLARSHIP - academic or scholarly achievement; knowledge acquired by study; learning.

SEXTANT - an instrument used mainly in navigation which can be used to measure the altitude of the sun or a star as an aid in determining the position of the observer.

SOCIAL STATISTICIAN - one who compiles statistics to be used to make predictions about societies.

SOLAR SYSTEM - the sun and all the heavenly bodies that move around it.

STENCH - disagreeable or offensive odor.

STROKE - sudden weakness or paralysis caused by a rupture or blockage of blood vessels in the brain; apoplexy.

SUICIDE - the act of intentionally taking one's own life.

SURVEYOR - one who surveys, or measures by some means, land.

TELESCOPE - an optical instrument for making distant objects appear nearer and larger, consisting of one or more tubes.

THEORIES - ideas that explain a group of facts or phenomena.

TREATISE - a book or other piece of writing dealing in a formal or systematic method with some subject.

TRIGONOMETRY - a branch of mathematics dealing with the relations between the sides and angles of triangles and the properties of these relations.

TURMOIL - state or condition of confused agitation or commotion.

UNIVERSE - all that exists, including the earth, the heavens, the galaxies, and all of space; the entire physical world.

UPHEAVAL - profound or violent disturbance or change.

VARIATION - something that differs slightly from another of the same kind.

WILL - a document giving the final settlement of a person's property after he or she dies.

110

ABOUT THE AUTHOR

Barbara Hooper Heckart has taught both elementary grades and graduate school classes. She has been an elementary school librarian since 1976. She gets her ideas for books children would like to read from their requests during library visits.

The author believes that the best part of writing is the research needed to make the subject live for readers.

Ms. Heckart enjoys history, genealogy, reading, travel, antiques, and finding bargains at sales and flea markets.